# Introduction

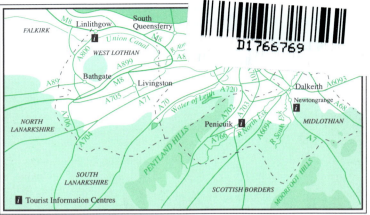

The area covered by this guide is comprised of the city of Edinburgh and the surrounding counties of Midlothian and West Lothian. It is bounded to the north by the cold waters of the Firth of Forth, and to the south by the Border hills. To the east is East Lothian and to the west Falkirk and Lanarkshire.

The two Lothians do not exactly fill their historical boundaries. The new unitary authority of Edinburgh has taken a little land from West Lothian and a good deal more from Midlothian, which has also lost the south-eastward spur which once reached into the Borders almost as far as Galashiels.

The area is dominated – historically, geographically and economically – by Edinburgh: Scotland's splendid old capital. The centre of the city is Scotland's greatest cultural relic: an architectural masterpiece of world renown. Beyond this lies the ring of suburbs, dormitory towns and industrial areas typical of any modern city.

The name is thought to be a reference to a fort built on a sheer rock by Edwin, king of Northumbria, in the 7th century ('Edwin's Burgh'). Edinburgh Castle now occupies the spot, and has long been the centre of the medieval part of the city – the Old Town – which stretches east from the castle to the Palace of Holyroodhouse *(7)*. On the far side of Princes Street Gardens are the terraces and squares of the Georgian New Town.

Edinburgh is built on seven hills. These provide most of the walking within the city boundaries – most famously on the rounded bulk of Arthur's Seat *(7)* – but there are also two lineal, long-distance paths starting within the city: the Water of Leith Walkway *(8)* and the towpath by the Union Canal *(4)*. The first of these follows the Water of Leith from the edge of the Pentland Hills, through the heart of the city and down to the old port of Leith on the Firth of Forth.

A number of villages have been swallowed up by the expanding city, notably Dean Village *(8)*, Corstorphine *(7)* and Cramond *(6,7)*. The latter – a charming village by the mouth of the River Almond – is a very old settlement. The Romans used the river mouth as a harbour and built a fort on the site, to act as a supply depot for the Antonine Wall which once stretched between the Forth and the Clyde.

*Palace of Holyroodhouse (Walk 7)*

Beyond the built-up area, the city's political boundaries have now spread to include towns such as Balerno and Currie *(8)* on the edge of the Pentlands, and the ancient burgh of South Queensferry *(5)*: a picturesque coastal town by the narrows of the Firth of Forth, now flanked by the massive road and rail bridges leading north into Fife.

Midlothian is comprised of the valleys of the Rivers North and South Esk (which converge at Dalkeith and join the Forth at Musselburgh as the River Esk) and the low land surrounding them. To the south-east the county boundary runs along the top of the escarpment of the Moorfoot Hills; to the south-west it encloses the greater part of the Pentland Hills.

This guide includes one walk across the moorland at the edge of the Moorfoots, the lineal walk over Fala Moor *(9)*, and one walk by the North Esk. The latter starts from the old mining village of Roslin (coalmining was once a major industry throughout this area), the site of the wonderful Rosslyn Chapel: a late medieval church of great beauty, surrounded by a mass of mysteries and exotic tales. It is a place well worthy of a visit on its own account *(10)*.

Most of the walks in Midlothian, however, are in the Pentland Hills *(11-23)*. The range rises abruptly to the south of Edinburgh, and the twin peaks of Caerketton and Allermuir, and the dry ski slope above Hillend (the longest in Europe) are clearly visible from much of the city *(11)*. For more general information on this splendid walking area, see the introduction to the Pentland walks before Walk 11.

As the built-up area of Midlothian is centred on the Esk, so the towns of West Lothian are mostly clustered around the River Almond. The largest of these is the new town of Livingston, near which there are parkland walks laid out along the riverbanks *(3)*. The southern part of the county is populous, with its past wealth based on mining and other heavy industries. The disappearance of many of these industries has been balanced by the introduction of a number of companies involved in the electronics sector.

The north of the county is more rural, but even here you will see signs of an industrial past, such as the shale bings: abrupt man-made hills made of the waste from the shale oil extraction process. Another industrial relic is the Union Canal, which was built to carry coal into Edinburgh and is now being made navigable once again, this time for recreational purposes *(4)*.

The canal winds westwards and passes through Linlithgow – the main town in the north of the county. Here there is one of the finest buildings in the area: the ruin of the 15th- and 16th-century Linlithgow Palace by the side of Linlithgow Loch *(1)*. This is evidence of West Lothian's older, aristocratic past, which can also be seen in the great houses at Hopetoun and Dalmeny *(5)*. For evidence of more ancient inhabitants, you might visit the remains of the ancient henge and cairns at Cairnpapple, or the Iron Age fort at Cockleroy *(2)*.

*Forth Rail Bridge (Walk 5)*

*A circuit of little Linlithgow Loch, passing the palace and church. The paths are clear and offer good views of the loch's wildfowl. Length: 2¹/₂ miles/4km; Height Climbed: none.*

O.S. Sheet 65

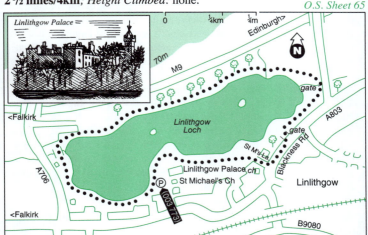

Linlithgow, the old county town of West Lothian, sits in the rolling farmland south of the Firth of Forth. At the heart of the town are the ruin of the royal palace (15th- and 16th-century), on the edge of the loch, and the splendid St Michael's parish church (15th-century).

From the centre of the town, follow the signs for the car park just to the west of the palace and church. A flight of steps leads down from the car park to the metalled path running by the side of the loch. Turn left along this.

There is no difficulty with the early part of the route, which follows the clear path as it runs round the western end of the loch and then on along its northern side. Beyond the eastern end of the loch the path leads up towards the public road. Shortly before this is reached there is a kissing gate on the right. Go through this and follow a clear, rough path across an area of grassland.

This path leads up to a gate leading onto the public road (Blackness Road). Turn right along the road, then right again down a narrow road (St Michael's Lane) by the parish church. This leads back down to the water, from where the shore path continues to the palace.

*Beecraigs is a 900 acre/370ha country park, largely covered by conifer woodland. The park has a variety of attractions, including three waymarked walks. One of these climbs out of the park to reach a low peak, providing fine views of West Lothian. Length: **up to 2 ¹/₄ miles/ 3.6km**; Height Climbed: **250ft/70m** (to top of Cockleroy). O.S. Sheet 65*

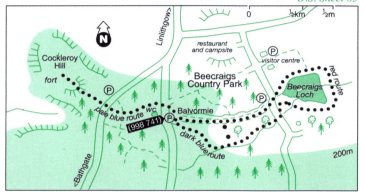

Beecraigs lies in the low, hilly farmland south of Linlithgow. To reach it, drive south from Linlithgow on Preston Road (off the main road, west of the town centre). This minor road leaves the built-up area and climbs the slope beyond.

The first road cutting off to the left (signposted) leads to the visitor centre, deer farm, fish farm, loch and restaurant. The second turn to the left (signposted for Balvormie) leads to the main car park for the walks. If you ignore these two junctions, you will reach the car park (to the right of the road) at the foot of the short version of the climb up Cockleroy.

Three colour-coded waymarked walks start from Balvormie car park. The shortest route (dark blue) takes a loop through the conifer woodland, passing the archery range on the way. The longest (red) starts on the same route, but continues beyond to go round little Beecraigs Loch, passing the fish farm.

The pale blue route heads off to the west, eventually exiting the woodland and climbing to the clear top of Cockleroy. Around the peak traces can still be seen of the old hill fort which once occupied the spot. It would have been a useful vantage point, as there are splendid views of West Lothian, Edinburgh and the Firth of Forth.

*Not so much a walk as a place to walk: two old estates in the valleys of the River Almond and its tributaries, with a mass of footpaths through the woods around the rivers. The Almond is crossed by a variety of splendid bridges. Length:* up to **4 miles/6.5km**; *Height Climbed:* undulating. *Visitor centre and barbecue sites.*

*O.S. Sheet 65*

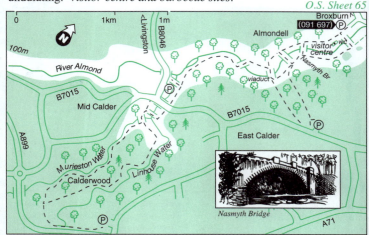

*Nasmyth Bridge*

Opened as a country park in the 1970s, Almondell and Calderwood covers around 230 acres of fine mixed woodland and includes excellent walks along about 4 miles/6.5km of paths by the River Almond and the Linhouse and Murieston Waters.

There are six bridges over the Almond – including the fine Nasmyth Bridge (1800) – plus the tall viaduct which once carried a spur railway line. In the valley there is also a splendid old iron aqueduct (1820): built as part of the feeder system for the Union Canal (Walk 4).

Almondell was once owned by the Erskine Earls of Buchan, and though Almondell House was demolished in the 1960s, the stable block remains and houses the visitor centre.

The park, which is surrounded by Mid Calder, East Calder and Livingston, can be entered from a number of points and has four car parks. To reach the North Car Park – the one nearest the visitor centre – follow the minor roads east from Pumpherston or Broxburn. For the positions of the other car parks, see the map.

*A long distance walk follows the towpath of this recently renovated canal. This section of the canal runs from Edinburgh to Linlithgow. Length: up to 22 miles/35km; Height Climbed: none.*

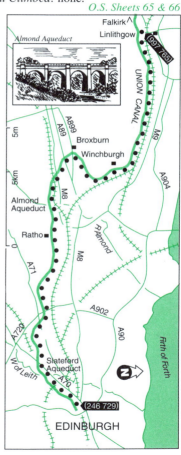

O.S. Sheets 65 & 66

The Union Canal, completed in 1822, was built to carry coal to Edinburgh. It has no locks for most of its length, and follows the 240 foot contour from Edinburgh to Falkirk. At its western end, a series of eleven locks once allowed traffic to drop in height to connect with the Forth & Clyde Canal. The canal was impassable for many years but it has recently been refurbished. The locks have been replaced by the splendid Falkirk Wheel and the Glasgow-Edinburgh canal link restored.

There is a towpath along the northern side of the canal, providing a completely flat walk which winds through the towns and countryside of West Lothian. There are no tunnels on this section, but there are two significant aqueducts – the Slateford Aqueduct in Edinburgh (carrying the canal over the Water of Leith – the Water of Leith Walkway can be joined at this point: *see* Walk 8) and the Almond Aqueduct, 2 miles/3km west of Ratho, which carries the canal over the River Almond.

The eastern end of the canal is at Edinburgh Quay (from the west end of Princes St, walk up Lothian Road, turn right into Fountainbridge, then left on Gilmore Park), but it can be joined at numerous places. The quietest walking is in the farmland east of Linlithgow.

*A splendid shoreline walk from the Forth Rail Bridge to the mouth of the River Almond, opposite the village of Cramond. Paths generally clear, but can be rough or damp in places. Length: up to* **10 miles/16km** *(there and back); Height Climbed: undulating. Ferry to Cramond may be operating: check in advance.* **No dogs.**

*O.S. Sheet 65*

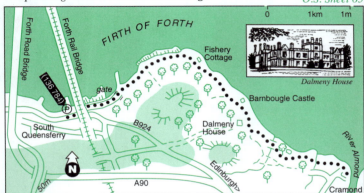

This splendid route can be walked in part or in whole. For the most part the route is perfectly clear.

If you are starting from South Queensferry, park by the shore at the eastern end of the town and walk towards the Forth Rail Bridge. As the road swings up to the right, turn left onto a metalled track running under the bridge. Follow this track along the shore to the Dalmeny Estate gatehouse.

Continue beyond this on the clear track by the shore, ignoring any turns to the right. The route passes through mixed woodland and provides fine views across the Firth to Fife.

You pass Fishery Cottage and

Barnbougle Castle (19th-century, on older foundations) and, just beyond the latter, the track emerges into parkland and Dalmeny House (1817; home of the Earls of Rosebery) comes into sight up to your right.

Follow the edge of the wood to your left, down towards the shore, to skirt round the edge of the golf course in front of the house. When a wood appears ahead, keep to its right. The path quickly becomes clear once again and continues the rest of the way to the mouth of the River Almond, opposite Cramond. Just before the river there is a Roman sculpture – the Eagle Stone – to the left of the path.

*A riverside walk through a narrow, wooded valley, starting from the pleasant coastal village of Cramond. Below the A90 the paths are clear; above, they can be damp in places. Length: **4 miles/6.5km**; Height Climbed: **100ft/30m**. Possible link with Walk 7 (B).*

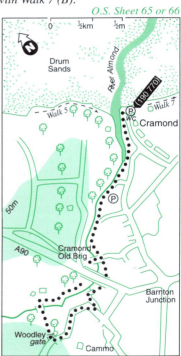

*O.S. Sheet 65 or 66*

Start this walk from Cramond, the heart of which is the little whitewashed village at the point where the River Almond joins the Firth of Forth. To reach it, turn north off the A90 at the Barnton junction, on the western edge of Edinburgh. Cramond is signposted, as are the two free car parks.

Whichever car park you have started from, walk down to the river and begin walking upstream, following the clear path signposted for Cramond Bridge/Cammo Estate. This fine path passes weirs, workmen's cottages and the old mills which the river once powered.

Follow the path up to the end of Cramond Old Brig. Do not cross this, but continue up the side of the river, passing under the A90 and continuing beyond. After a short distance you cross a small burn, then turn left, up a narrow path between buildings, to join a metalled road.

Turn right and follow the road until, opposite the entrance to Cammo, there is a little gate, with a house entrance just to the right ('Woodley'). Go through the small gate and follow a path down a narrow line of trees to reach a single-span stone bridge over the river.

Cross this and turn right (you will see a number of planes on the walk: this bridge is almost in line with the runway of nearby Edinburgh Airport). When you reach Cramond Old Brig cross over and return to the start by the original route.

O.S. Sheet 66

*The city of Edinburgh is fortunate in having a number of particularly fine green areas and long paths within its boundaries. The Water of Leith Walkway and the Union Canal towpath are dealt with elsewhere (Walks 8 and 4). The entries in this section are further suggestions of areas to be explored. They range from a gentle stroll along the esplanade at Cramond to a steep hill climb on Arthur's Seat.*

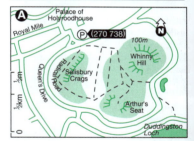

## A Holyrood Park & Arthur's Seat

The large mound of Arthur's Seat and the sharp edge of Salisbury Crags are classic features of the Edinburgh skyline. They are located in Holyrood Park, which is best accessed through the gates beside the Palace of Holyroodhouse, at the foot of the Royal Mile.

The park is around 650 acres/260 ha. in extent, and the peak of Arthur's Seat – the basalt plug of an old volcano – is 823ft/251m high.

You may wander at will around the park, and there is also an extensive path network. The two obvious walks are along the 'Radical Road' at the foot of the Salisbury Crags and the climb up Arthur's Seat (the two can be combined). The views of the city from these paths are magnificent. If you wish to extend your walk, you might choose to visit the little village of Duddingston (with its pleasant old inn) by the side of Duddingston Loch.

## B Cramond

The walk south from Cramond is described elsewhere in this guide (*see* Walk 6). The little whitewashed village at the mouth of the Almond (turn north off Queensferry Road at the Barnton junction) is worth exploring on its own account, with its small harbour, Roman remains (there was a fort here), tower, church (15th-17th century) and inn.

In addition, there is a pleasant walk along the esplanade, towards Granton, and the possibility of walking the tidal path out to Cramond Island (just under a mile: you will need to check the state of the tide locally before attempting this).

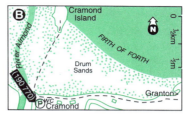

## C Hermitage of Braid/Blackford Hill

Blackford Hill, a low, grassy peak rising above the southern part of the city, is the site of the Royal Observatory. The Hermitage of Braid is a narrow, wooded glen which runs along its southern edge. The various paths exploring the two are connected and make for very pleasant walking; surprisingly quiet in the shaded glen and with fine views from the open hilltop.

There is a car park at the gate by Blackford Pond (drive south down Morningside and turn west

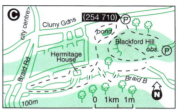

onto Cluny Gardens). Alternatively, there is a pleasant walk in along the Hermitage, starting at Braid Road and following the Braid Burn past the Gothic mansion which gives the Hermitage its name.

## D Corstorphine Hill

Corstorphine Hill is a low, wooded ridge in the western part of the city. There are a number of access points to the various paths around the hill, but perhaps the easiest approach is from Corstorphine, about 3 miles west from the centre of the city on the A8 road for Glasgow.

Corstorphine, with its fine medieval church, was once a separate village, but was long ago swallowed up by its larger neighbour. From the main street, drive (or walk) up Clermiston Road, then turn fifth right onto Cairnmuir Road. At the end

there is a small car park and a gate leading onto the hill.

It is about 1 mile/1.5km to the far end of the hill (Queensferry Road). Near the start of the ridge you will pass a Gothic tower, built as a monument to Sir Walter Scott.

# 8 Water of Leith Walkway ————————— A/B/C

*A series of linked, waymarked paths following the Water of Leith between Balerno and the port of Leith, passing through the heart of Edinburgh on the way.* **Length:** *up to* **13 miles/21km**; *Height Climbed:* **500ft/150m** (Leith to Balerno).

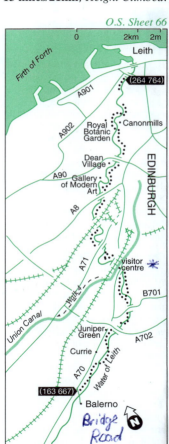

O.S. Sheet 66

The Water of Leith starts amongst the hills around Harperrig (*see* Walk 23), flows along the western flank of the Pentlands then continues through Edinburgh to end at Leith Docks.

The path along it has been gradually improved until it is now unbroken between Leith and Balerno. A walk along its length shows an extraordinary cross-section of the city and its suburbs.

Having said this, the path can be accessed at many points, and most people will be content to walk only part. The section of greatest interest is the 2 miles/3km stretch from Canonmills to the Scottish National Gallery of Modern Art (*see* map). This passes the 19th-century artisans' houses at the Colonies, the splendid landscaped parkland around St Bernard's Well, the Dean Bridge and Dean Village.

Other highlights include the approach to the newly invigorated harbour at Leith, the woodlands around Craiglockhart and Colinton Dells and a fine view of Murrayfield (the home of Scottish rugby).

More information on the river and its paths can be found at the Water of Leith Visitor Centre on Lanark Road – open daily, 10.00-16.00 (Mon-Sun), refreshments available (*see* map).

*Currie hill road, Slateford rail, Kingsknowe rail EH14 2JX*

*A moderate lineal walk over flat moorland, providing fine views over the Lothians. Birdwatching opportunities. Length: up to **5 miles/8km** (one way); Height Climbed: **300ft/90m** (north to south), **200ft/60m** (south to north). Route clear, but rough and damp in places.*

*O.S. Sheet 66*

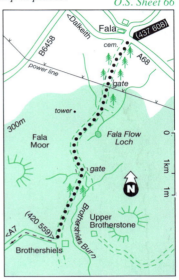

This is a true lineal walk, with no alternative returns. Given the difficulty of parking at the south end of the route, it will be best to walk as far as one wishes from the north and then return by the same path.

Fala is a tiny village, just below the escarpment of the Lammermuirs. To reach it, drive 8 miles south from Dalkeith on the A68. Just beyond the turn-off for the village to the left, turn right onto a track signposted for the cemetery. There is limited parking on the left-hand side of the road.

Walk on along this road, with a stand of larch to the left, to reach a gate. Go through the pedestrian gate beside it and continue. At the end of a second plantation a track swings off to the left. Ignore this and carry straight on across the moorland on a clear track.

This is a heather moor, rich in peat and the accompanying flora. Duck and other water birds may be seen on little Fala Flow Loch, to the left of the track. The stump visible to the right of the track is all that remains of Fala Luggie: a tower built around 1600. On the horizon to your left you can see a line of wind generators and, to the left of a stand of trees, Soutra Aisle: the remains of a church built around 1164.

Shortly before crossing a burn there is a gate, beyond which the cover gradually changes from moor to rough grazing land. This may be a good place to turn round. If you wish to complete the crossing, go through the gate and continue towards the trees visible ahead. The rough, wet track runs through these then continues down to the farm at Brothershiels. Here it joins a minor road which leads down to the A7.

*A sequence of rough paths and tracks around the narrow, wooded valley of the River North Esk, passing the ruin of Rosslyn Castle and the splendid Rosslyn Chapel. Length:* **4½-6 miles/7-9.5km**; *Height Climbed:* undulating.

*O.S. Sheet 66*

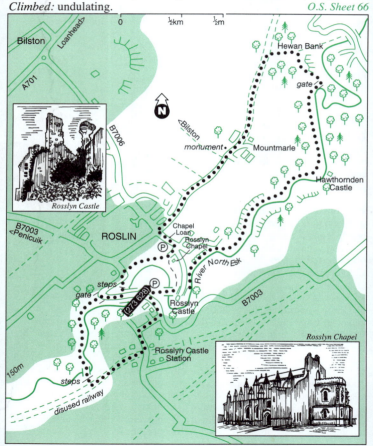

Bilston

Loanhead>

A701

B7006

N

<Bilston
monument
Mountmarle

Hewan Bank

gate

Hawthornden
Castle

*Rosslyn Castle*

B7003
<Penicuik

ROSLIN

Chapel
Loan
Rosslyn
Chapel

P

River North Esk

P

steps
gate

(273 628)

Rosslyn
Castle

B7003

150m

steps

Rosslyn Castle
Station

disused railway

*Rosslyn Chapel*

Roslin is a small mining town to the east of the Pentland Hills. To reach it, drive 2 miles north from the centre of Penicuik on the A701, then turn right onto the B7003. This road skirts the western side of the town. At the main junction (with the B7006) continue along the B7003. There is a car park to the left of the road just after it crosses the river.

Walk out of the back of the car park and look for a sign for a footpath, pointing to a footbridge over the river. Cross this and follow the path up the slope beyond. Note the path heading off to the right, passing under a stone bridge, but for the moment keep straight on to reach Rosslyn Chapel. (Begun in the mid-15th century, this is one of the most splendidly decorated and historically interesting churches in Scotland.)

Drop back down the slope and turn left, beneath the bridge – the entrance to the semi-ruined Rosslyn Castle. A fine path, rough in places, now leads down the glen. Along the way you will notice the 17th-century Hawthornden Castle (*see* map).

Beyond Hawthornden, continue by the river until it bends hard right and a bank comes across ahead. At this point, go through a kissing-gate in a fence and turn left shortly beyond, through a gap in a fence. Climb a slope to reach a T-junction. Turn left here, along Hewan Bank (SSSI). This is eroded in places and it may be necessary to follow an alternative route (watch for signs).

Either way, continue to a further T-junction in a line of woodland. Turn left here, along a clear track. Follow this track to Mountmarle (note the monument to the battle of Roslin, 1303). Carry straight on, ignoring the tracks to right and left, and follow the minor road beyond into Roslin.

Turn left onto Chapel Loan, then turn right, just before the Chapel. At the next junction, instead of turning left (the way you came up before) carry straight on. Follow the edge of the wood to the public road.

Turn left, following the pavement at first and then a steep flight of steps leading down to the side of the road just before it crosses the river. For the shorter route, turn left here, back to the car park. For a slightly longer walk, turn right, up the pavement by the public road, until a gateway is reached to the left at a hairpin bend.

Go through the pedestrian gate and follow the clear track beyond, passing through woodland above the North Esk and noting the lades, weirs and ruined mills along this stretch of the river. This wood was once the site of the largest gunpowder mill in Scotland.

Turn left on a bridge over the river. A short distance beyond a flight of steps climbs up to the left. Climb these then drop down again to join the line of the old railway. Turn left along this and follow it as far as the old Rosslyn Castle Station. A road crosses the line at this point. Climb onto this and head left (north-west) to reach the B7003, then turn left again to return to the car park.

# Walks Edinburgh, Midlothian & West Lothian

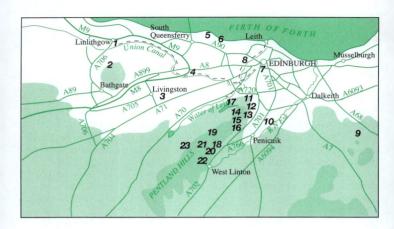

## Grades

**A** ........ Full walking equipment required

**B** ........ Strong walking footwear and waterproof clothing required

**C** ........ Comfortable walking footwear recommended

[**B/C** ... **B**-grade route if walked in its entirety;
           **C**-grade if walked in part]

*Published by:* Hallewell Publications, The Milton, Foss, Pitlochry, Perthshire PH16 5NQ
*Printed by:* Halcon Printing Ltd, Stonehaven

# Walks Edinburgh, Midlothian & West Lothian

# The Pentland Hills: Introduction

The Pentlands constitute one of the finest low-level hill walking areas in Scotland. They are a narrow range of moorland and grass hills, peppered with reservoirs, extending south-westwards from the southern edge of Edinburgh. The hills are largely given over to sheep grazing, with some grouse shooting on the moors towards the south of the range.

The northern end of the range has been designated the Pentland Hills Regional Park. The headquarters are at Boghall, and there is a Ranger Centre at Harlaw and an information centre at Flotterstone.

The map opposite shows the area of the hills covered in this guide, the main approach roads, the whereabouts of the numerous car parks and the routes of the various signposted and accepted paths over and between the hills.

With this map (or the map distributed by the Regional Park) and the correct Ordnance Survey sheets, experienced walkers will have no problem picking out potential routes – the paths are generally clear and their ends well signposted.

For those who are new to the hills, the authorities have signposted four short circular walks, starting from Flotterstone, Bonaly, Hillend and Harlaw, which give a gentle introduction to the area.

For those who wish to try something a little more challenging, the following pages describe a number of alternative walks which, between them, cover most of the area's path network. Possible connections are mentioned; others will suggest themselves as you become better acquainted with the hills.

All of the routes described have their charms, but:

For the best **views of Edinburgh** you should climb Caerketton or Allermuir, behind Hillend (Walk 11).

For the best **hill walking**, follow Walk 16, which climbs a line of five of the highest peaks in the range.

For the best **low-level route**, follow Walk 15, up the valley of the Logan Burn, through dramatic Green Cleugh and down to Bavelaw.

For the **quietest walking** (some of these routes can be busy, particularly at weekends), try one of the stiffer moorland routes at the southern end of the area (Walks 21 and 23).

Other objects of specific interest include the dry ski slope at Hillend (Walk 11) and the excavated hill fort and earth house at Castlelaw (Walk 12). If you enjoy a pint or something to eat at the end of a walk, there are good inns at Hillend, Flotterstone. Carlops and West Linton.

For further information about the Park, contact the Rangers at Boghall: *tel:* 0131 445 3383

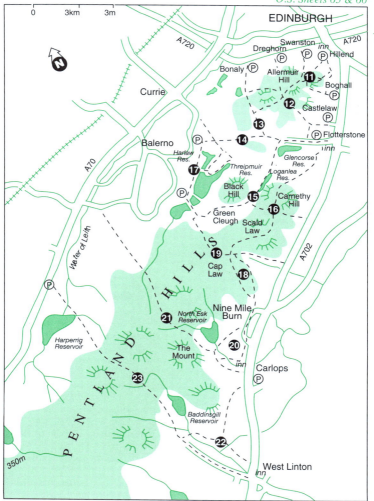

EDINBURGH

A720

A720

Dreghorn

Swanston · inn

Hillend

Bonaly (P)

Allermuir Hill

(P) (P) (P)

Boghall

Currie

⓫

(P)

⓬

Castlelaw

(P)

⓭

(P) Flotterstone

Balerno

(P)

⓮

inn

Harlaw Res.

⓯ Threipmuir Res.

Glencorse Res.

(P)

Loganlea Res.

Black Hill

⓱

Carnethy Hill

(P)

⓯

⓰

Green Cleugh

Scald Law

Water of Leith

H I L L S

⓳

Cap Law

⓲

(P)

Nine Mile Burn

⓴

A702

⓴

P E N T L A N D

North Esk Reservoir

㉑

Harperrig Reservoir

The Mount

inn

Carlops

(P)

㉓

Baddinsgill Reservoir

㉒

350m

West Linton

inn

0   3km   3m

N

*A network of paths at the northern end of the Pentland Hills. This area includes the dry ski slope at Hillend, the pretty village of Swanston, and the peaks of Allermuir and Caerketton, which provide unrivalled views over Edinburgh. Paths are rough and steep in places. Length:* **2-5 miles/3-8kms**; *Height Climbed:* up to **1000ft/300m** (Boghall to top of Allermuir Hill).

*O.S. Sheet 66*

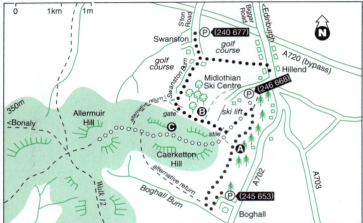

There are three car parks on this network of paths. To reach **Hillend**, drive south from Edinburgh on the A702. Shortly after crossing the City Bypass there is an entrance to the Midlothian Ski Centre to the right. Turn up this road.

To reach **Swanston**, turn south off Oxgangs Road onto Swanston Road. This leads over the Bypass to the car park, just before the village.

To reach **Boghall**, follow the A702 2 miles beyond the Bypass and turn right at the signs for Boghall Farm.

**A Hillend to Boghall:** This is a short, low-level route, but even from this path the views over Edinburgh and East Lothian are superb: Arthur's Seat, North Berwick Law, the Bass Rock, the Lammermuirs.

After you have reached the car park at Hillend, turn left, shortly beyond the entrance, into the smaller overflow car park. The path for this route starts from the far end of this car park.

This part of the Pentlands is criss-crossed with paths, but the route is quite straightforward. Follow the clear path, contouring along a slope of grass, gorse and birch. A clear path climbs up from the left and continues uphill to the right, signposted for the Capital View Walk (symbol). Ignore this and continue. A second signposted path cuts off to the right. Ignore this once again.

The path, fainter now, joins a fence to the left with trees beyond. Continue along this until you join the clear path running up Boghall Glen. A turn to the left at this point will take you down to the car park at Boghall.

The easiest return from this point is back the way you came. Alternatively, if you turn right onto the clear path up the glen it will lead you to the ridge between Caerketton and Allermuir and to alternative paths to Swanston and Hillend (*see* below).

**B Hillend to Swanston:** There is a high route and a low route to Swanston: a pretty hamlet of thatched and whitewashed cottages. This route starts by the high, steep route and comes back the easier way.

Start as for Boghall (*see* above), but this time turn right at the first junction with the Capital View Walk.

This leads you over a low hill and up to the fence which runs across the hill above the top of the ski slope. There is a stile over the fence with a signpost just before it.

Turn right (signposted for Swanston) and walk across the slope with the fence and the ski slope down to your right. When the fence cuts off to the right you follow the path down and across the slope to rejoin the fence at the top of the T Wood.

Continue along the path, which shortly passes through a gate. Just beyond this there is a junction. Go right here, down the shallow valley of the Swanston Burn.

At the foot of the village there is a sign pointing right for Lothianburn. Follow this level track to the main road (signposted for Swanston back the way) and turn right. After a short distance turn right again at the entrance to the Ski Centre.

**C Caerketton & Allermuir:** This is the steepest of the short walks from Hillend. Start as above, but when you cross the fence which runs above the ski slope, carry straight on; climbing the slope on the path signposted for Caerketton.

The path leads to the top of the hill (magnificent views) then drops down before climbing again to the slightly higher Allermuir. For an alternative return, take the rough, steep path which leads down from the dip between the hills to the Swanston Burn.

*Swanston Village*

_A lineal hill crossing, largely on clear paths, including a chance to see an excavated earth house._ **Possible danger from neighbouring rifle range: watch out for red flags.** _Length:_ **3 miles/5km** (one way); _Height Climbed:_ **550ft/170m** (south to north); **900ft/270m** (north to south).

*O.S. Sheet 66*

Drive 3 miles south from the edge of Edinburgh on the A702 and turn right at the sign for Castlelaw. The car park is by the farm at the end of the minor road.

The path is signposted for Dreghorn. Shortly after its start it passes the excavated earth house. This has been left open so that you are able to get inside the structure.

Continue climbing up the clear path, with the rifle range (please note warnings) and Glencorse Reservoir down to your left. Ignore paths to right and left. When the path reaches the second low pass there is a cattle grid and a path climbs to the right. Ignore this and carry straight on.

At the next pass there is a more significant junction. A short, steep climb to the right will lead up Allermuir, while the path to the left provides a possible alternative return route via Phantom's Cleugh and Glencorse (_see_ map). To complete this route, carry straight on: dropping down the glen of the Howden Burn on a clear path.

When the path reaches a hut there is a signposted junction. Cross the burn here, as shown, and follow the rough, grassy path down to the public road. (**NB:** this is an army training area, please stick to the paths).

**If you are starting from Dreghorn**, turn off the A720 (City Bypass) at the signs for Colinton. Get to the Pentlands (south) side of the road and then onto the slip road leading back onto the A720 for west bound traffic. Turn left off this on the minor road for 'Dreghorn Ranges'. There is parking by the path end.

*A lineal crossing by a low hill pass. Paths clear but rough; fine views over Edinburgh. Length:* **4 miles/6.5km**; *Height Climbed:* **500ft/150m** (either way).

*O.S. Sheet 66*

Drive south from the southern edge of Edinburgh for 3 miles on the A702 and turn right at Flotterstone. Just beyond the inn, on the right, there is a car park.

Walk on up the metalled road, signposted for Glencorse Reservoir. Continue on this road, ignoring paths to either side, until it dog-legs left at a bend in the reservoir to your left. Look for the signpost here and turn right, off the road, on the path for 'Colinton by Bonaly'.

Follow the clear track past a conifer plantation to another junction. Go right here, for Bonaly, and follow the path over a shoulder of Harbour Hill. At the burn on the far side a path cuts off to the right by a fence. Ignore this and continue up to the low hill pass at the head of the burn.

Beyond the pass views begin to open up of Edinburgh and the Forth Bridges. When the path reaches a conifer plantation, go through a gate to the left (a path for Allermuir continues), pass through the trees (with Bonaly Reservoir to your left) then continue on the clear path beyond.

When you reach the junction at the edge of the next band of conifers, go straight on, down the hill, to reach the car park above Bonaly.

**If you are starting from Bonaly**, Turn off Woodhall Road (an extension of Colinton Road) onto Bonaly Road. Follow this to its end to reach the car park, on the way passing Bonaly Tower: a 19th-century structure built for Lord Cockburn in the baronial style. Carry straight on along the line of the road to start the walk.

*A lineal hill crossing over a low pass.  Paths clear; fine views.  Length:*
**4 miles/6.5km** (one way)*; Height Climbed:* **550ft/160m** (south to north)*;*
**330ft/100m** (north to south).

*O.S. Sheet 66*

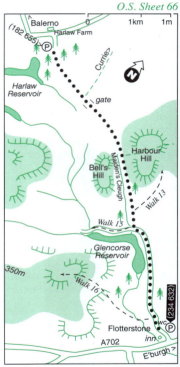

Drive south from the southern edge
of Edinburgh for 3 miles on the A702
and turn right at Flotterstone.  Just
beyond the inn, on the right, there is
a car park.

Walk on up the metalled road,
signposted for Glencorse Reservoir.
Continue on this road, ignoring paths
to either side, until it dog-legs left at
a bend in the reservoir to your left.
Look for the signpost here and turn
right, off the road, on the path for
'Balerno by Harlaw'.

Follow the clear, rough path by a
stand of conifers to another junction.
Continue on the path up the glen,
signposted as before, towards the
hill pass – Maiden's Cleugh – visible
ahead.

Beyond the pass the path continues
clearly; dropping down to a gate in
a dyke.  On the far side there is a
junction, with a path to the right for
Currie.  For this route, however, keep
to the left; continuing through grazing
and then fenceless arable land, with
the trees around Harlaw Reservoir
visible down to the left, to the car
park in a narrow line of conifers.

**If you are starting this walk
from the Harlaw end**, drive south
from Edinburgh on the A70 and take
the first turn to the left signposted for
Balerno.  Once on this road turn first
left, signposted for Marchbank, then
left again onto Harlaw Road.  Follow
this road for about a mile until it
dog-legs sharp left.  Turn first right
beyond this to reach the car park.

This walk is signposted for
Glencorse Reservoir.

*A lineal track through, rather than over, the Pentland Hills, following clear tracks and metalled roads and passing through the narrow defile of Green Cleugh.  Length:* **7 miles/11km** *(one way); Height Climbed:* **450ft/140m** *(east to west);* **250ft/75m** *(west to east).*

*O.S. Sheet 66*

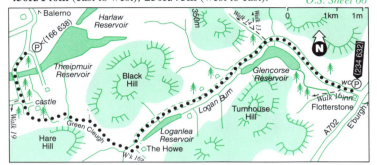

To start from Flotterstone, drive south from the southern edge of Edinburgh for 3 miles on the A702 and turn right at Flotterstone.  Just beyond the inn, on the right, there is a car park.

Start walking along the metalled road which continues beyond the car park, signposted for Glencorse Reservoir.  Follow this up to the reservoir and continue by the water's side; the road dog-legging to the left as the valley winds its way into the hills.

Continue up the valley beyond Glencorse Reservoir, passing Loganlea Reservoir and the white house beyond ('The Howe').  Just beyond the latter there is a signposted junction.  A climb up to the left leads onto the hill tops and a possible alternative return (*see* Walk 16).  For this route, however, carry on up the valley, signposted for Balerno.

The path swings right into the narrow pass of Green Cleugh.  At the watershed there is a dyke with a stile and a gate.  Cross the stile and continue, dropping down towards the trees around Bavelaw Castle (private residence).

Follow the clear track to the left of the wall around the castle grounds.  This leads down to a junction at the top of a long, tree-lined drive.  If you carry straight on at this point, then turn first left at the sign for the path to Nine Mile Burn, this leads to a possible return *via* the hill tops (*see* Walks 19 and 16).  To complete this route, however, walk down the driveway.  Threipmuir car park is a little beyond the reservoirs on the right.  The centre of Balerno is a further two miles along the road.

*The classic hill walk in the Pentlands: a lineal route crossing five peaks. Paths rough and steep in places. Views splendid. Length:* **7 miles/11km** (one way)*; Height Climbed (total for five peaks):* **2300ft/700m** (north to south)*;* **2000ft/610m** (south to north).

*O.S. Sheet 66*

These are the peaks – Turnhouse Hill, Carnethy Hill, Scald Law, East Kip and West Kip – which flank the A702. There is little doubt about the route between the peaks once you are up there: a rough, steeply undulating path, with each top visible from the last. The main question is which route to take to get up there.

**If you are starting from the northern end**, drive south from the southern edge of Edinburgh for 3 miles on the A702 and turn right at Flotterstone. Just beyond the inn, on the right, there is a car park.

Walk on along the metalled road, watching for a sign to the left for Scald Law. This leads you across the Glencorse Burn and onto a clear path leading up a grassy ridge to the first peak: Turnhouse Hill. Cross the next four peaks then drop down to Nine Mile Burn as for Walk 18.

For an alternative return, make use of the Kirk Road path (between Carnethy Hill and Scald Law) and the path along the valley of the Logan Burn (*see Walk 15*).

**To reach Nine Mile Burn**, drive 8 miles south from the southern edge of Edinburgh on the A702 and turn right at the signs.

To reach the first peak – West Kip – follow the directions for Walk 18 as

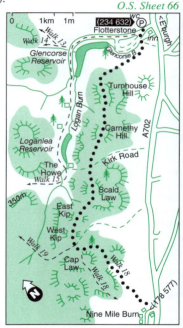

far as the watershed, then turn right up the steep path to the top.

There are no short return loops (walking by the A702 is not recommended). For a longer return, you might use Walks 15 or 19, or a combination of the two (around 17 miles/27kms for the walk in total).

*A series of linked paths by two reservoirs, passing through woodland and grazing land.  Length:* up to **4 miles/6.5km**; *Height Climbed:* up to **100ft/30m**.

*O.S. Sheet 66*

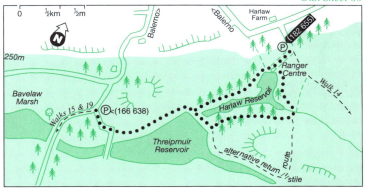

To reach the car park at Harlaw, drive south from Edinburgh on the A70 and take the first turn to the left signposted for Balerno.  Once on this road turn first left, signposted for Marchbank, then turn left again on Harlaw Road.  Follow this road for about a mile until it dog-legs sharp left.  Turn first right beyond this to reach the car park.

(To reach the alternative car park at Threipmuir, ignore the turn onto Harlaw Road and continue to the end of the road.)

Walk out of the car park, in the direction of the hills, and turn right immediately on a metalled road with the woods to your right.  This quickly brings you to the Ranger Centre at the end of Harlaw Reservoir.

The easiest walk is simply to follow the path through the trees around Harlaw (signposted as the Harlaw Woodland Walk).  The paths are perfectly clear and there is no climbing involved.

From the far end of the reservoir it is possible to continue by Threipmuir to the alternative start at Threipmuir car park, then return by the same path.

If you want an alternative return from the west end of Harlaw, cross the causeway between the two reservoirs, as if circuiting Harlaw (signposted for Black Springs).  At the junction, however, continue by a narrowing arm of Threipmuir.  Follow this until, just before its end, there is a stile over the metal fence to the left.  Cross this and follow the rough path beyond down to the eastern end of Harlaw.

*A moderately difficult loop on faint paths, rough and damp in places. Some navigation necessary. Length:* **4 miles/6.5km**; *Height Climbed:* **550ft/170m**.

*O.S. Sheet 65 or 66*

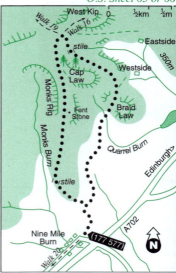

To reach Nine Mile Burn, drive 8 miles south from the southern edge of Edinburgh on the A702 and turn right at the signs. There is room to park at the point where the minor road cuts to the left.

At the parking area there is a gate and a sign for the path to Balerno. Walk along the foot of the field beyond, then turn left up the slope with the dyke to your right. At the top of the field there is a stile. Cross this and turn right. At the next stile there is a choice. For this route go straight on (Braid Law).

Follow the foot of the field then swing left to a gate and stile in the far corner. Cross the stile and follow the rough path beyond, with the Quarrel Burn down to the right.

The path crosses the burn then climbs up to a low watershed behind Braid Law. Follow the path down the slope beyond and it quickly swings left, up the valley. At one point there is a junction of tracks. An arrow indicates the track ahead and to the left. Follow that track: past some woodland (stile) and on up to the watershed.

Just as you approach the fence which runs through the watershed, double back to the left along a clear, rough path. This runs along below the grassy ridge to your right, with the area of woodland down to the left.

The path climbs onto the ridge and splits. Keep right at this point, heading due south down the nose of land between the valleys of Monks Burn and Quarrel Burn. On the way, you pass the Font Stone (probably a socket for a cross which has since been removed).

Drop down to a fence with a stile over it. Turn left beyond this and walk on with the fence to your left. At the foot of the slope you join your original track at the junction passed before.

*A moderately difficult lineal path over the Pentland Hills, following rough paths, unclear in places.  Length:* **5 miles/8km** (one way, to Threipmuir car park)*; Height Climbed:* **550ft/170m** (south to north)*;* **650ft/200m** (north to south).

*O.S. Sheet 65 or 66*

To reach Nine Mile Burn, drive 8 miles south from the southern edge of Edinburgh on the A702 and turn right at the signs.  There is room to park at the point where the road cuts inland.

Start this route as for Walk 18. Follow this up to the junction on the watershed below West Kip and take the clear track signposted for Balerno; dropping down into the shallow valley of the upper Logan Burn.

The path drops gently through the heather moorland, then swings to the right to cross the burn and climb to a low watershed beyond.  Go through a gate in the dyke and continue beyond, dropping down through heather then grazing land to pass to the left of a square conifer plantation west of Bavelaw Castle (private).

Follow the path down to a tree-lined metalled track and turn right. You quickly reach a junction.  Turn left here, down the main driveway. Threipmuir car park is just beyond the reservoir on the right-hand side.  If you are continuing to Balerno, add a further 2 miles/3km to the distance.

**If you are starting from Threipmuir**, drive south from Edinburgh on the A70 and take the first turn to the left signposted for Balerno.  Turn first left, signposted for Marchbank, and follow this road to the car park at its conclusion.

Continue walking along the driveway which continues beyond the road.  Pass the reservoir and climb to a junction.  Turn right and follow the signs for Nine Mile Burn (*see also* Walk 18).

*A moderate loop through farmland and hill grazing, following rough paths, tracks and the public road. There is an inn at Carlops. Length:* **5 miles/8km**; *Height Climbed:* **550ft/160m**.

*O.S. Sheet 65*

To reach Nine Mile Burn, drive 8 miles south from the southern edge of Edinburgh on the A702 and turn right at the sign. There is room to park at the point where the minor road cuts to the left.

Walk on along this minor road. Just beyond the last of the houses the entrance road for Spittal Farm opens up to the right, signposted as the path to Buteland. As you approach the buildings a track heads off to the right. Follow this, keeping left at a junction to join a clear track above the farm. This crosses a small burn and climbs towards the watershed behind Patie's Hill.

On the watershed there is a cattle grid. Beyond this the path splits, with the main track heading off to the right. Ignore this and carry straight on along a clear, grassy track. After a very short distance the fence to the left cuts away and the path splits again. Cut off the main track onto a fainter path which heads down and across the slope to the left.

This leads down to the dam of the North Esk Reservoir. Cross this to reach a signposted junction by a cottage. Go straight on: Carlops.

Follow the clear access road down the valley. Just beyond the house at Fairliehope there is a choice: either continue down the metalled road or turn left at the sign; dropping down by the burn to a footbridge, crossing and turning right to reach Carlops.

Either way, once you have reached the A702 in Carlops turn left. Watch for a sign for a footpath to Nine Mile Burn, starting up steps to the left. Follow this path parallel to the main road to join the minor road along which you started. Continue along this to return to the start.

*A low hill crossing, through heather moorland and grazing land, passing North Esk Reservoir along the way. Paths generally clear, but rough and wet in places. Length:* **6 miles/9.5km** (one way)*; Height Climbed:* **350ft/110m** (south to north)*;* **600ft/180m** (north to south).

*O.S. Sheet 65*

Carlops is a small village with an inn, 11 miles south of the southern edge of Edinburgh on the A702.

Walk to the northern end of the village and look for a sign for the footpath to Buteland. Follow this, beside a hedge at first then on up the side of a burn in a narrow valley.

After a short way there is a bridge to the left, Cross this and follow the faint path up a field with Fairliehope to the right and a tributary burn down to the left. This joins the metalled track at a signposted junction. Turn right, signposted for Buteland.

Follow this clear track up to North Esk Reservoir (in wet weather there may be a diversion indicated, avoiding the muddy ground around the end of the dam). It follows the west side of the reservoir then continues up the glen of the Henshaw Burn to a gate in a dyke at the watershed. ('The Bore Stane' is the name given to the rock outcrop in the stand of trees to the left).

Beyond this a clear path leads down the shallow slope. After 1½ miles/2.5kms the path runs down the side of a conifer plantation to join the access drive to Listonshiels (in a stand of trees to the left). Continue straight down the drive to join the minor public road.

**If you are starting from the**

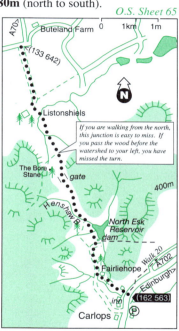

*If you are walking from the north, this junction is easy to miss. If you pass the wood before the watershed to your left, you have missed the turn.*

**northern end**, drive to Grid Ref 129 655 on the A70 and turn onto a minor road signposted as a footpath to Carlops. Turn right at the T-junction and park by the drive entrance which heads off first left (133 642), where there is room for three or four cars. Start walking up the driveway and then follow the signs.

**22)** *A moderate loop around a pleasant valley on paths of varying quality and a quiet public road. Length:* **5 miles/8km**; *Height Climbed:* **250ft/75m**. **23)** *A lineal route crossing the Pentland Hills, passing through grazing land and moorland. Path generally clear, but rough and wet in places. Length:* **8 miles/13km**; *Height Climbed:* **650ft/200m** (south to north); **500ft/150m** (north to south).

*O.S. Sheet 65*

West Linton is a village on the A702, some 14 miles south of the southern edge of Edinburgh.

**Walks 22 & 23)** Park in the village and walk up to the main road. Opposite the Gordon Arms there is a sign for a path to Carlops, leading up The Loan. Follow this up through houses and into farmland.

This road ends at a junction with another vehicle track. Turn right along this, then first left (signposted for Cauldstane Slap). Follow this past Stonypath Farm and on beyond (very muddy in wet weather).

As the track approaches a tributary burn it swings uphill to the right. At this point a grassy path carries straight on. Follow this, crossing the burn and continuing up the glen to the wall at the edge of Baddingsgill House grounds. Turn left here, as directed, dropping down to the Lyne Water, crossing at a footbridge and climbing the far slope to reach the public road.

**Walk 22)** Turn left here to return to West Linton.

**Walk 23)** For the the longer route, turn right and follow the road, and the track which continues beyond, onto the moorland and up to the watershed.

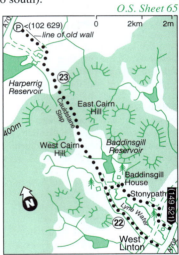

Continue on the rough path which drops down the shallow slope beyond to the marshy ground around Harperrig. Follow the waymarkers to avoid the farm and continue up to the car park by the A70.

**If you are starting from Harperrig,** drive 4 miles south of Balerno on the A70 and watch for the sign for the West Linton path to the left of the road. The car park is just beyond (locked after 7.30pm).